These Are My Senses

What Can I Taste?

Joanna Issa

Raintree is an imprint of Capstone Global Library Limited, a company incorporated in England and Wales having its registered office at 7 Pilgrim Street, London, EC4V 6LB – Registered company number: 6695582

www.raintreepublishers.co.uk
myorders@raintreepublishers.co.uk

Edited by Siân Smith
Designed by Richard Parker and Peggie Carley
Picture research by Tracy Cummins
Production by Victoria Fitzgerald
Originated by Capstone Global Library Ltd
Printed and bound in China by RR Donnelley Asia

ISBN 978 1 406 28367 9
18 17 16 15 14
10 9 8 7 6 5 4 3 2 1

British Library Cataloguing in Publication Data
A full catalogue record for this book is available from the British Library.

Acknowledgements
We would like to thank the following for permission to reproduce photographs: Corbis: © Ocean, 15; Dreamstime: © Artranq, 10; Getty Images: Cultura/Lisbeth Hjort, 8; iStock: © Rdvan Çelik, 13; Shutterstock: © Eduard Stelmakh, 5, © EMprize, 6, 20 left, 22 left, back cover, © Gelpi JM, 7, © isarescheewin, 4, 21 right, © jerrysa, 12, © Johan Larson, 9, 22 right, © Karen H. Ilagan, 17, © Kesu, 14, 21 left, © Lana Langlois, 18, 20 right, © Olga Miltsova, 16, © Vitaly Korovin, 11, © Zurijeta, 19

Cover photograph reproduced with permission of Corbis, © Sam Diephuis.

Every effort has been made to contact copyright holders of material reproduced in this book. Any omissions will be rectified in subsequent printings if notice is given to the publisher.

Contents

What can I taste?

I taste a strawberry.

It is sweet.

I taste a lemon.

It is **sour**.

I taste popcorn.

It is **salty**.

I taste a chilli pepper.

It is spicy.

I taste candyfloss.

It is sweet.

I taste limes.

They are sour.

I taste olives.

They are salty.

I taste chocolate.

It is sweet.

Quiz: Spot the difference

Which foods are sour?

The lemons and limes are sour foods.
The strawberry and chocolate are sweet.

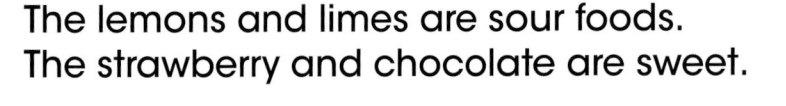

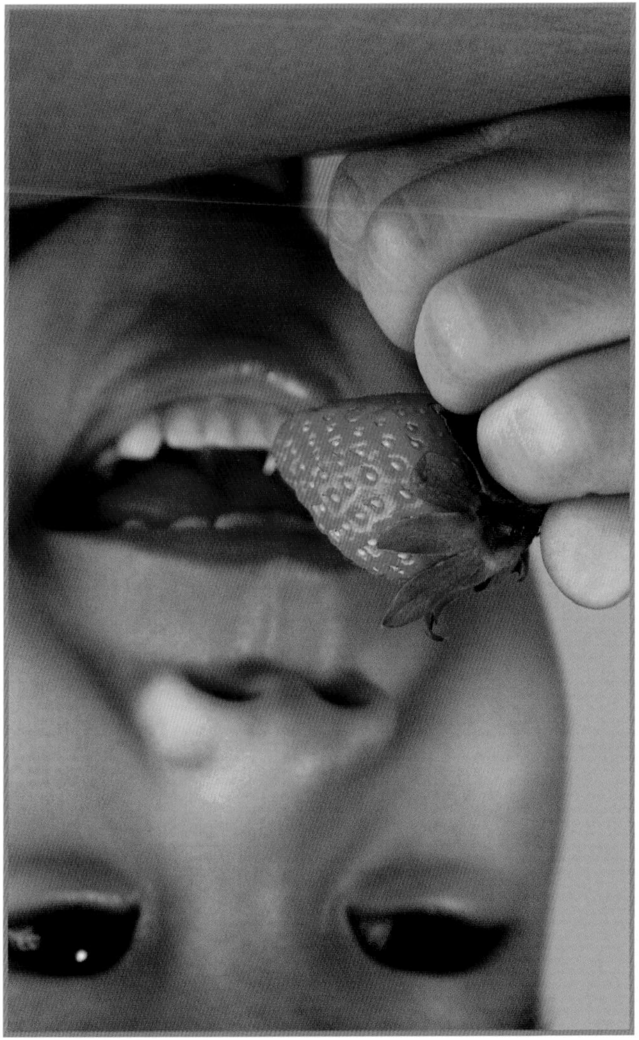

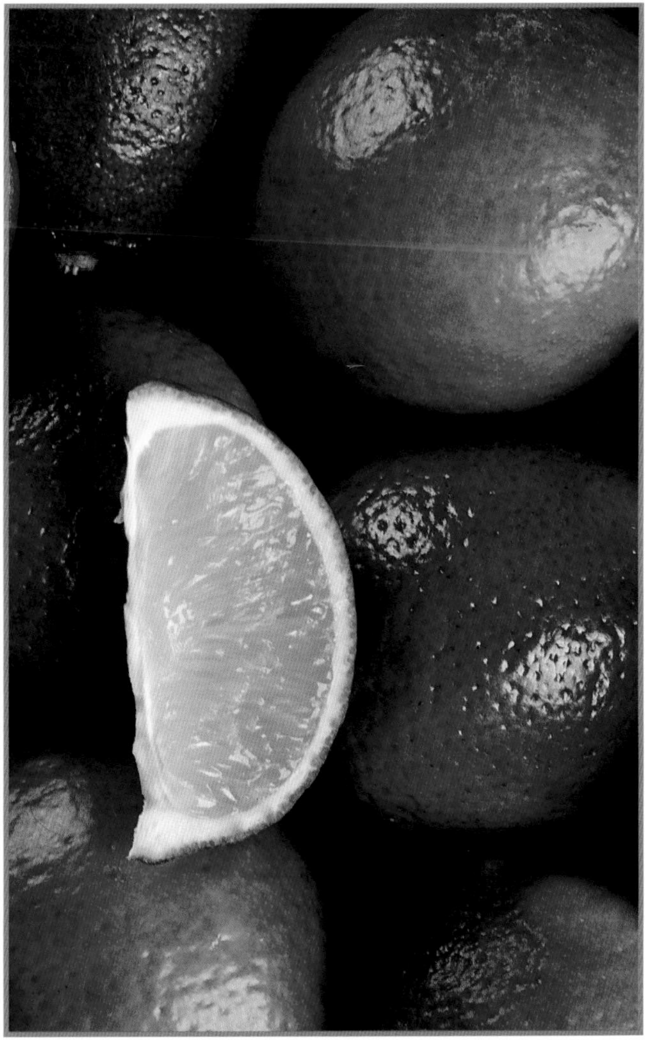

Picture glossary

 salty

 sour

Index

Notes for teachers and parents

BEFORE READING

Building background:
Ask children to name a favourite food. Why do they like it? Has it always been their favourite food? Why do they think different people like to eat different things?

AFTER READING

Recall and reflection:
Which foods taste salty (popcorn, olives)? Which foods taste sour (lemons, limes)? Which foods taste sweet (strawberries, candyfloss, chocolate)? Do children prefer foods that taste salty or sweet?

Sentence knowledge:
Ask children to look at page 5. How many sentences are on this page? What type of punctuation mark is used at the end of the sentence?

Word knowledge (phonics):
Encourage children to point at the word *taste* on page 4. Sound out the four phonemes in the word $t/\bar{a}/s/t$. Ask children to sound out each phoneme as they point at the letters and then blend the sounds together to make the word *taste*. Challenge them to say some words that rhyme with the word *taste* (paste, waste).

Word recognition:
Ask children to find the word *sweet* on page 5. How many more times can they find it in the book?

EXTENDING IDEAS
Make four columns on a piece of paper. At the top of each column, write one of these headings: sweet, sour, salty, spicy. Give children food magazines or advertisements to look through to find examples of different foods. Ask children to cut out pictures and paste them in the correct spots on the chart. Then ask children to decide which is their favourite taste.

In this book

Topic

tastes and senses

Sentence stems

1. I taste _____.
2. It is _____.
3. They are _____.

High-frequency words

a

are

I

is

it

they